MAR -- 2018

D0392098

A Note to Parents

DK READERS is a compelling program for beginning readers, designed in conjunction with leading literacy experts, including Dr. Linda Gambrell, Distinguished Professor of Education at Clemson University. Dr. Gambrell has served as President of the National Reading Conference, the College Reading Association, and the International Reading Association.

Beautiful illustrations and superb full-color photographs combine with engaging, easy-to-read stories to offer a fresh approach to each subject in the series. Each DK READER is guaranteed to capture a child's interest while developing his or her reading skills, general knowledge, and love of reading.

The five levels of DK READERS are aimed at different reading abilities, enabling you to choose the books that are exactly right for your child:

Pre-level 1: Learning to read
Level 1: Beginning to read
Level 2: Beginning to read alone
Level 3: Reading alone
Level 4: Proficient readers

The "normal" age at which a child begins to read can be anywhere from three to eight years old. Adult participation through the lower levels is very helpful for providing encouragement, discussing storylines, and sounding out unfamiliar words.

No matter which level you select, you can be sure that you are helping your child learn to read, then read to learn!

DK

LONDON, NEW YORK, MUNICH,
MELBOURNE, and DELHI

Editor Emma Grange
Designers Jon Hall, Sandra Perry
Senior Pre-Production Producer Jennifer Murray
Producer Louise Minihane
Managing Editor Elizabeth Dowsett
Design Manager Ron Stobbart
Publishing Manager Julie Ferris
Art Director Lisa Lanzarini
Publishing Director Simon Beecroft

Reading Consultant
Linda B. Gambrell, Ph.D.

Dorling Kindersley would like to thank: Randi Sørensen and
Robert Stefan Ekblom at the LEGO Group and J. W. Rinzler,
Leland Chee, Troy Alders, and Carol Roeder at Lucasfilm.

First American Edition, 2014
15 10 9 8 7 6 5
Published in the United States by DK Publishing
4th Floor, 345 Hudson Street, New York, New York 10014

011–196543–July/14

Page design copyright © 2014 Dorling Kindersley Limited

LEGO, the LEGO logo, the Brick and Knob configurations,
and the Minifigure are trademarks of the LEGO Group.
© 2014 The LEGO Group
Produced by Dorling Kindersley Limited under license
from the LEGO Group.

© 2014 Lucasfilm Ltd. & ™. All rights reserved.
Used under authorization.

All rights reserved under International and Pan-American
Copyright Conventions. No part of this publication may be
reproduced, stored in a retrieval system, or transmitted in any
form or by any means, electronic, mechanical, photocopying,
recording, or otherwise, without the prior written permission
of the copyright owner.
Published in Great Britain by Dorling Kindersley Limited

DK books are available at special discounts when purchased in bulk
for sales promotions, premiums, fund-raising, or educational use.
For details, contact: DK Publishing Special Markets, 4th Floor,
345 Hudson Street, New York, New York 10014
SpecialSales@dk.com

A catalog record for this book is available
from the Library of Congress.

ISBN: 978-1-4654-2031-2 (Paperback)
ISBN: 978-1-4654-2030-5 (Hardcover)

Color reproduction in the UK by Altaimage
Printed and bound in China

All other images © Dorling Kindersley
For further information see: www.dkimages.com

Discover more at
www.dk.com
www.starwars.com
www.LEGO.com/starwars

Contents

4   Saving the galaxy

6   Sith Lords

8   Secret weapon

10   Vader's past

12   Skywalker and friends

14   Jabba the Hutt

16   Jabba's collection

18   Tatooine mission

20   In the rancor pit

22   Escaping the Sarlacc

24   Grand Jedi Master

26   The last Jedi?

28   Rebel attack

30   On Endor

32   Meeting the Ewoks

34   Shield generator

36   Battle of Endor

38   Sith vs. Jedi

40   Father and son

42   Final act

44   Galaxy celebrations

46   Glossary

DK READERS

READING
3
ALONE

LEGO STAR WARS

RETURN OF THE JEDI™

Written by
Emma Grange

Mon Mothma

General Madine

Saving the galaxy

Here are some very brave rebels.
They are fighting to free the galaxy
from the control of the evil Empire.
They may not look like much, but
they have great courage and have
faced many battles without fear.

Rebel Pilot

Admiral
Ackbar

Rebel
Commando

After their last battle with the
Empire, the rebels were scattered
throughout the galaxy. Now they
are looking for a way to defeat
the Empire once and for all.

One of the rebel leaders, Mon
Mothma, is planning their next
move. Soon, she will summon all of
the rebel pilots, troopers, and fighters.

Sith Lords

The ruler of the Empire is the sinister Sith Lord Darth Sidious, also known as the Emperor. He has an equally villainous apprentice named Darth Vader. The Sith seek power and control for themselves.

Red Guard

Darth
Sidious

Darth
Vader

The Emperor and his apprentice have a vast army to serve them. Look out for the Royal Red Guards and the scary stormtroopers!

Darth Sidious thinks that it will be easy to defeat the rebels. He has a secret plan to make sure that the Empire cannot be beaten…

Stormtroopers

Death Star II

Secret weapon

This moon-shaped object may look familiar. It is called the Death Star and it is the Empire's secret weapon. In fact, it is their second Death Star. The first Death Star was destroyed in an act of great daring by the rebels. This time, Darth Sidious and Darth Vader are taking no chances. The new Death Star is protected by an impenetrable, super-strong shield system, making it almost impossible to destroy.

The rebels will have to find a way to turn off the shield!

Vader's past

Before Darth Vader joined the Sith he was a Jedi named Anakin Skywalker. Anakin used the Force for good, in order to protect the galaxy. However, Darth Sidious persuaded him to join the dark side, promising him he would find greater power there.

Anakin
Skywalker

Jedi Knight
The Jedi also use the Force but, unlike the Sith, they use it for good and never for evil.

When Anakin became the Sith
Lord Darth Vader, he didn't know
he was leaving behind a son and a
daughter. That son is the rebel Luke
Skywalker, who is now
training to be a Jedi
Knight. Luke and Vader
have fought once
before. In order to
defeat the rebels,
Vader must
either turn
Luke to
the dark
side—or
destroy
him.

*Darth Vader looks
fierce and frightening.
He has a dark and
secret past.*

Skywalker and friends

Luke Skywalker is determined to defeat the Sith and free the galaxy from the Empire. He also wants to save his father and bring him back to the light side of the Force.

First, he must rescue his friend Han Solo, who is being held prisoner on the planet Tatooine.

Luke
Skywalker

Princess
Leia

Han Solo has saved Luke's life more than once. Now Luke has a chance to save him in return!

For this mission, Luke is joined by a collection of Han's closest friends: the rebel Princess Leia, the Wookiee Chewbacca, the two droids R2-D2 and C-3PO, and Han's old friend Lando Calrissian.

C-3PO

R2-D2

Chewbacca

Lando Calrissian

Frozen solid

Han has been frozen in a material called carbonite to prevent him from escaping.

Jabba the Hutt

This slimy, green slug-like creature is crime lord Jabba the Hutt. Jabba has amassed great wealth and power on the planet Tatooine by stealing and smuggling. He employs many people to do his dirty work for him. He expects those people to always obey him. If they don't, then they had better watch out!

Han Solo used to work for Jabba, but he ended up owing him a lot of money. For revenge, Jabba plans to hold Han prisoner forever.

Many guards protect Jabba from all of his enemies and keep him safe in his palace.

Jabba's collection

Jabba loves collecting things, especially spice, money, and valuable objects. He owns a vast collection of droids. He also likes collecting people and keeping them as slaves.

At Jabba's command, some of his slaves must perform to entertain him. A girl named Oola dances, while a small, blue musician named Max Rebo plays music with a special instrument called a red ball organ.

The prize of Jabba's collection is a meat-eating monster called the rancor. Anyone who displeases Jabba is thrown down to the rancor pit.

Oola

red ball organ

Max Rebo

trapdoor

Jabba's rancor lives in a pit beneath the palace. On Jabba's instruction, a trapdoor opens and people fall down below!

Tatooine mission

Han's friends have several sneaky plans to try to free him from the clutches of Jabba the Hutt.

First they send R2-D2 and C-3PO with a message. Luke offers the droids as a gift. Greedy Jabba takes the droids, but refuses to talk about releasing Han!

Then Princess Leia arrives disguised as a bounty hunter. In the middle of the night, Leia frees Han from the carbonite, but is soon discovered by Jabba. As punishment, Leia will become Jabba's slave.

Jabba's palace

Han is relieved to be freed from the carbonite. His imprisonment has made him feel weak and temporarily unable to fight!

Luke arrives to talk to Jabba face to face. His Jedi mind tricks only make Jabba laugh. When Luke tries to blast Jabba, he falls through the trapdoor into the rancor pit!

Bounty hunters
Bounty hunters work for the highest bidder, often capturing their prey for a large reward.

In the rancor pit

The hideous rancor was once given to Jabba as a birthday present. It has huge teeth and claws, and is kept in a pit beneath the palace.

When Luke falls into the rancor pit he must use all of his Jedi powers and some creativity to escape. Using a handy bone, he tricks the carnivorous creature and then manages to destroy it before he is eaten.

Not everybody is pleased that Luke has escaped the fearsome beast. Jabba is sad to have lost his pet, and now he must think of another way to rid himself of his unwelcome visitors.

Guard

Escaping the Sarlacc

Far out in the Tatooine desert, Jabba has something bigger and scarier waiting for Luke Skywalker and his friends.

The Sarlacc creature lives buried deep in the desert sands. Can you see its beak and tentacles above the sand? The Sarlacc is always hungry. Jabba plans to feed it his enemies as a small snack!

Lando Calrissian

Jabba's Desert Skiff

Unfortunately for Jabba, nothing goes according to plan. Luke attacks Jabba's guards with the lightsaber that R2-D2 had hidden, while Leia frees herself from Jabba. Lando and Han blow up Jabba's barge, and the lucky Sarlacc eats many of Jabba's guards. Delicious!

Guard

Lightsaber

Sarlacc

Grand Jedi Master

Reunited once more, the rebels are ready to face the Empire. However, Luke knows that he must complete his training with Jedi Master Yoda on the swampy planet Dagobah. Then he will truly be a Jedi.

Yoda is more than 900 years old and has seen many battles. He is still strong in the Force, but now he is old and tired. He knows that it is time to leave this life and become one with the Force.

Jedi teacher
Yoda has watched over Luke Skywalker from afar for many years. Now he knows that the young Jedi is ready to take on the Sith by himself.

Long-lost sister
Luke is shocked to learn that he has a twin sister—his rebel friend Princess Leia!

The last Jedi?

After Yoda's death, Luke is visited by the Force ghost of his old friend Obi-Wan Kenobi. It was Obi-Wan who first told Luke he could be a Jedi, before he let himself be defeated by Darth Vader.

Obi-Wan has some last words of wisdom for Luke. He confirms that Darth Vader is Luke's father. Luke feels that Vader is not all evil.

He also warns Luke to be wary of the Emperor, who plans to lure him to the dark side. The temptation might be great. Beware the dark side, Luke!

Rebel attack

Back on board their Star Cruiser base, *Home One*, the rebels make plans to destroy the new Death Star.

Mon Mothma gives Han Solo a special mission to blow up the shield generator that is protecting the Death Star.

Mon Mothma

Admiral Ackbar

Hologram of the Death Star

The shield generator is on the forest moon of Endor and is guarded by Imperial forces. The rebels must sneak past the Empire's fierce stormtroopers and scout troopers to destroy the shield.

If they are discovered or defeated, their mission will be a failure!

Lando Calrissian

General Madine

On Endor

Scout trooper

Down on Endor's moon, the rebels soon run into trouble. Some scout troopers have wandered far from their base on a mission. They are not pleased to bump into the rebels!

Luckily for the rebels, the troopers are not very clever. As Luke and Leia chase after the scout troopers on their speeder bikes, one of them flies into a tree! Unfortunately, during the chase, Leia is separated from her friends.

Forest moon
This small moon is covered in lush forests. It orbits the planet Endor, and is usually a peaceful place.

Speeder bike

For now, Han and Luke must continue without her.

Wicket

Ewok warrior

Chief Chirpa

Meeting the Ewoks

As the rebels travel further into the woods, they fall into an Ewok trap! Camouflaged among the trees on the forest moon, these small furry creatures are expert hunters.

The Ewoks plan on eating the rebels, but after some persuading, the rebels are freed and reunited with Leia—who has already made friends with one Ewok named Wicket.

Ewok leader
Chief Chirpa leads the Ewok tribe. He and the Ewoks decide to help the rebels.

Teebo

Logray

The curious Ewoks are not sure what to make of the rebels at first. The Ewoks could show them the way to the shield generator, but it would be safer to not get involved.

Eventually, the rebels, with help from C-3PO, persuade the Ewoks to help them and free their planet from the Empire forever.

33

Shield generator

The Ewoks lead the rebels to the shield generator. The shield protects the Empire's giant weapon and can be disabled only by blowing up the bunker and adjoining satellite dish.

Darth Sidious sends a small army of stormtroopers to surround the rebels.

The rebels have brought the droids R2-D2 and C-3PO along for this special task. However, it looks like Darth Sidious knew of the rebels' plans all along. It was all part of the Sith Lord's evil trap.

Droid friends
The loyal droid R2-D2 is programmed to work with computers. He could work faster if his friend C-3PO stopped bothering him!

The clever Ewoks use everything
they have in the fight against
the Empire.

Battle of Endor

The Ewoks may look cute, but they fight fiercely. When their planet is threatened, they do everything they can to help the rebels.

Some Ewoks gather sticks
and stones to throw at the
stormtroopers. Others operate
catapults to launch large
rocks at the approaching
forces. Well done, Ewoks!

Now that the scout troopers
and stormtroopers have all been
vanquished, the droids can blow up
the Death Star's shield generator.
The rebels' grand plan is nearly
complete.

Sith vs. Jedi

Luke has to confront Darth Sidious. He knows Sidious will try to persuade him to join the Sith, but Luke is ready to refuse him.

Darth Sidious is angered by Luke's refusal. The Jedi is no longer useful to him and so he blasts him with deadly Force lightning. Luke is no match for Darth Sidious's dark side powers.

Force lightning
The Force is a powerful energy. Darth Sidious uses it to create deadly Force lightning that can fatally harm his opponents.

Darth Vader is torn. He turned from the Jedi to become a Sith many years ago, but he cannot stand aside and watch his son be destroyed. Which side will he choose? Is there still some good left in Darth Vader?

Father and son

In the end, Darth Vader chooses love for his son over fear of his Sith Master. At great risk to himself, he grabs Darth Sidious and throws him down a deep reactor shaft. Darth Sidious is destroyed in a deadly explosion.

Darth Vader's dying wish is for Luke to remove his mask so he can see his son with his own eyes.

Darth Vader has saved Luke and destroyed the Emperor. These selfless actions finally free him from the dark side of the Force, but at a great cost. He has been fatally injured by the Emperor's Force lightning.

X-wing Fighter

Final act

Meanwhile, Lando Calrissian is leading an air attack in space against the Empire from onboard Han Solo's ship, the *Millennium Falcon*. Imperial pilots fly after him in their TIE fighters, but they are not fast enough to catch Lando or the rebel pilots in their X-wing starfighters.

Millennium Falcon

With the shield down, Lando is
able to fly right into the very center
of the Death Star's core. From the
inside he then causes an explosion
that blows it into thousands of tiny
pieces. Lando and Luke flee to safety
just in time!

Galaxy celebrations

The galaxy is free at last from the control of the Empire! The menace of the Sith has also been destroyed.

People from different planets across the galaxy celebrate the good news. The combined courage of the rebels, Jedi, droids, and some small Ewoks helped to save the galaxy.

Luke is glad to be reunited with Han and his sister, Leia. He knows that he could not have done anything without them, and the help of Jedi Masters Obi-Wan Kenobi and Yoda.

The galaxy is peaceful once more, but who knows what challenges the future holds?

Glossary

Adjoining
Next to or connected to.

Amassed
Gained or collected many things.

Apprentice
Student or pupil.

Bunker
Strong building, used to keep things safe.

Camouflaged
Disguised to resemble and blend in with the surroundings.

Carnivorous
Creature that eats an entirely meat-based diet.

Confront
Question or challenge.

Droid
Metal robot.

Empire
Group of nations ruled over by one leader, who is called an Emperor.

Galaxy
Group of millions of stars and planets.

Generator
Machine that creates power, usually electrical.

Hologram
3-D image of someone or something that is not there, used as a way to communicate.

Impenetrable
Impossible to pass through or enter.

Imperial
Belonging to the Empire.

Jedi
Someone who uses the Force to protect people and keep the peace.

Lightsaber
A weapon made of pure Force energy, used like a sword.

Lure
Persuade someone to go somewhere or do something with the promise of a reward.

Menace
A threat. Something likely to cause danger.

Rebel
Person who rises up to fight against the current ruler.

Scout
Soldier sent on ahead to check for signs of the enemy and report back.

Selfless
Unselfish, to think of and act for others before oneself.

Sinister
Frightening, evil.

Sith
Someone who uses the Force for selfish reasons and to gain power.

Skiff
Shallow, flat-bottomed vehicle.

Smuggling
Illegally moving valuable goods from one place to another and selling them for a profit.

Snare
Catch someone inside a trap.

Summon
Gather or call a group of people together.

Temptation
Feeling of wanting to do something that sounds attractive.

TIE Fighter
Type of starfighter flown by the Empire's forces.

Vanquished
Utterly defeated.

X-wing
Type of starfighter flown by rebel forces.

Index

Anakin 10, 11

bounty hunters 18, 19

C-3PO 13, 18, 35
catapults 37
carbonite 14, 18, 19
Chewbacca 13
Chief Chirpa 32, 33

Dagobah 24
dark side, the 10, 11, 27, 41
Darth Sidious 6, 7, 9, 10, 34, 35, 38, 39, 40, 41
Darth Vader 6, 9, 10, 11, 27, 39, 40, 41
Death Star 8, 9, 28, 37, 40, 43
droids 16, 35, 37, 44

Emperor 6, 7, 27, 41
Empire 4, 5, 6, 7, 9, 12, 24, 32, 33, 34, 36, 42, 44
Endor 29, 30, 36
Ewoks 32, 33, 34, 36, 37, 44

Force, the 10, 12, 25, 27, 41
Force Ghost 26, 27
Force lightning 38, 40, 41
forest moon 29, 30, 32

galaxy 4, 5, 10, 12, 44, 45

Han Solo 12, 13, 14, 15, 18, 19, 23, 28, 29, 42, 45
hologram 28

Home One 28

Imperial forces 29, 42

Jabba 14, 15, 16, 17, 18, 19, 20, 22, 23
Jedi 10, 11, 19, 20, 24, 25, 27, 38, 39, 44, 45

Lando 13, 18, 22, 23, 42, 43
Leia 12, 13, 18, 19, 23, 26, 45
light side, the 12
lightsaber 23, 38
Luke 11, 12, 13, 18, 19, 20, 21, 23, 24, 25, 26, 27, 38, 39, 41, 43, 45

Max Rebo 16, 17
Millennium Falcon 42, 43
Mon Mothma 4, 5, 28

Obi-Wan 26, 27, 45
Oola 16, 17

palace, Jabba's 15, 17, 18, 20

R2-D2 13, 18, 35
Rancor 16, 17, 19, 20, 21
red guards 7
rebels 4, 5, 9, 11, 20, 22, 24, 28, 29, 30, 31, 32, 33, 34, 35, 36, 37, 42, 44

Sarlacc 22, 23
scout troopers 29, 30, 31, 37
Sith 6, 10, 11, 12, 25, 27, 38, 39, 40, 44

shields 9, 28, 29, 33, 34, 43
shield generator 29, 33, 34, 37
skiff 22, 23
speeder bikes 30, 31
stormtroopers 7, 29, 32, 34, 37

Tatooine 12, 14, 18, 22
TIE fighters 43

Wookiee 13

X-wing fighters 42

Yoda 24, 25, 27, 45

DK

Here are some other DK Readers you might enjoy.

Level 3

LEGO® *Star Wars*® Revenge of the Sith™
The Jedi must save the galaxy from the Sith!
Will Anakin fall to the dark side?

LEGO® Legends of Chima™: Race for CHI
Jump into battle with the animal tribes as
they fight to get their claws on the CHI!

Angry Birds™ *Star Wars*® Lard Vader's Villains
Discover a band of naughty villains! Meet Lard Vader and
the Empire Pigs as they try to take control of the galaxy.

LEGO® Monster Fighters: Watch Out, Monsters About!
Join Dr. Rodney Rathbone and his Monster Fighters
as they try to stop the evil Lord Vampyre.

LEGO® Friends: Summer Adventures
Enjoy a summer of fun in Heartlake City with
Emma, Mia, Andrea, Stephanie, Olivia, and friends.